By Eamonn Corrigan

Published by The Child's World®
800-599-READ • childsworld.com

Photography Credits
NASA/NASA, Cover, title page, 21, 30-31; Youness Bensaid/Shutterstock.com, 4-5; zuhdison art/ Shutterstock.com, 7; NASA, 9 (top), 29 (top left); NASA, 9 (bottom); Domenichini Giuliano/ Shutterstock.com, 11, 29 (bottom right); Rawpixel.com/Shutterstock.com, 13, 29 (bottom left); JPL-Caltech/Space Science Institute/NASA, 15, 29 (top left); Artsiom P/ Shutterstock.com, 16-17; NASA/Penn State University/Wikimedia Commons, 19; Cmglee/ Wikimedia Commons, 23; ESA, 25; JPL-Caltech/NASA, 27

ISBN Information
9781503877931 (Reinforced Library Binding)
9781503878549 (Portable Document Format)
9781503879089 (Online Multi-user eBook)
9781503879621 (Electronic Publication)

LCCN
2025938217

Printed in the United States of America

ABOUT THE AUTHOR

Eamonn Corrigan has been teaching curious kids about science for over a decade, which means he's answered approximately 47,000 questions about why the sky is blue and whether penguins have knees. (The answers: light scattering and yes!) When he's not writing children's books or in the classroom, Eamonn loves getting his hands floury while baking bread, whipping up delicious meals in the kitchen, and completely dominating his friends and family at board games (okay, maybe he loses sometimes, too).

Table of Contents

AS YOU READ, LOOK FOR

DIPTHONGS AND SILENT LETTERS

CHAPTER 1

The Cosmic Journey Begins

Have you ever looked up at the night sky and wondered about everything out there? The mysteries of the cosmos? What are those small glowing points of light we usually call stars? The dark sky above us is full of amazing objects. Some are big, and some are small. Some are close to Earth. Others are far away. Even with our most powerful telescopes, there is still so much to discover.

But what if we could go visit these objects? Would you make that choice? Imagine the excitement and joy of leaving Earth's soil. Enjoying the noise of the rocket. Flying far beyond our **solar system**. Going where no human has ever gone before in the name of science. What would you discover floating in the cosmic void?

Leaving Earth, we would first see our closest neighbors. These are the thousands of **satellites** that humans have built and launched into space. And don't forget our nearest neighbor, the Moon! It is always looking down on us, circling around us everywhere we go. Flying outward, who knows what will be found? We'll visit the most interesting objects in our own solar system. But our solar system is not alone. We are surrounded by hundreds of billions of similar star systems. Our **galaxy** is huge! There is so much out there to discover. So strap in, and enjoy the journey. It's time to discover the most interesting objects in space.

A person stands beneath the wonders of the night sky.

SATELLITES: EARTH'S SPACE SUPPORT SYSTEM

Our rocket roars as we plow through the clouds. The sky turns from blue to black. We've left the atmosphere and entered space! Look around us now. We're not alone out here.

Thousands of human-made satellites orbit our planet. Different countries and companies have launched these amazing machines. These satellites play very important roles in our daily lives. Some are as small as a toaster. Others are bigger than a school bus!

There are communication satellites. They help people talk to or text someone on the other side of the world. Research satellites help scientists collect information about how our world works. Weather satellites help predict tomorrow's weather. They also help us understand how our climate is changing.

GPS satellites help with navigation and positioning. There are currently only 31 satellites that run the entire GPS system. Everyone using their smartphone for directions needs these satellites. Every airplane and every ship employ just these 31 satellites. It's incredible what they can do!

All satellites are truly a marvel of modern engineering. So much of our daily lives depend on these orbiting heroes. In the future, we'll have even more satellites. There were about 6,000 satellites orbiting Earth in 2022. By 2030, there may be over 60,000! But how will this affect our ability to travel into space?

To use GPS, three different satellites are needed to determine exactly where you are on Earth.

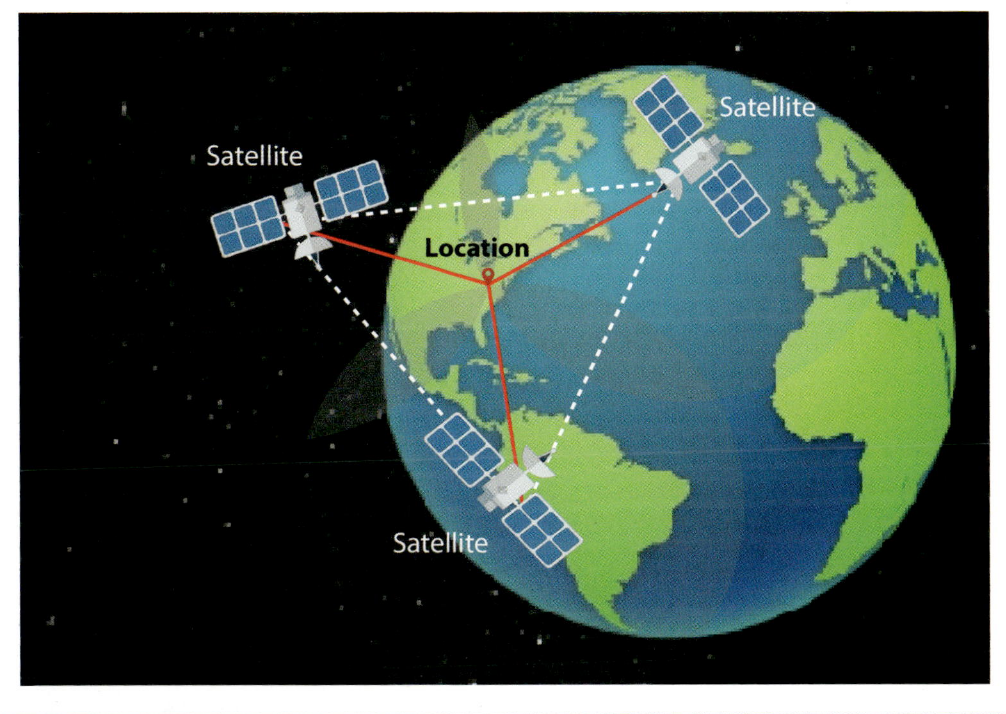

SPACE JUNK

Not everything floating out there is helpful. There's a lot of junk, too. Old rocket parts drift around us. Broken satellites still orbit aimlessly around the planet. Even scraps of paint and spare screws float through space.

If you think this isn't a problem, read on. Space junk can be very dangerous. Everything orbits Earth at incredible speeds. In low Earth orbit, satellites move at about 18,000 miles per hour (28,968 kilometers per hour). Modern rifles only shoot bullets at about 2,500 mph (4,023 km/h).

Think about how much damage a small bullet can do. Now imagine a broken satellite the size of a car. If it's moving seven times faster.... Ouch! That's like a bomb. Astronauts at the *International Space Station* (ISS) must worry about this. They must often avoid space junk. Space travelers use small rockets to move out of the way.

Thankfully, scientists are working on solutions. They are trying to clean up our orbit. They're also trying to prevent future space junk. They know we must act quickly. If we're not careful, we could drown in space junk.

DID YOU KNOW?

In 2021, the Chinese satellite *Yunhai-1* broke apart after being struck by a piece of space debris! Crumbs rained down to the ground below.

NASA works hard to track all known pieces of space junk to avoid collisions.

This photo shows a cracked window on the ISS after it was struck by a piece of space junk.

OUR TRUSTED COMPANION: THE MOON

Looking back at Earth, we watch it slowly grow smaller and smaller. We're now 238,000 miles (370,149 kilometers) from our loyal home. From here, Earth looks like a blue marble all alone out in space. But we're not alone out here. The Moon is always with us.

The Moon has been circling Earth for more than four billion years! It is known as the brightest point in the night sky. It's hard to miss. It looks light gray with darker gray spots all over it.

These dark spots are scars from the Moon's rough past. Many were caused by impacts long ago. Countless asteroids and comets have crashed into the Moon's surface. They leave behind large explosion **craters**.

Unlike Earth, the Moon doesn't have volcanos. It used to, but not anymore. On Earth, our surface is constantly changing because of volcanos. Hot **lava** erupts and then cools in the air into solid rock. This smooths out old scars. It's like getting regular facelifts over millions of years. The Moon keeps all its scars forever. That's why we can see so many craters.

But the Moon used to have volcanos too. The extra-large dark spots we see are called **mare**. These were once giant lakes of lava. Old volcanos erupted and filled huge craters. When the lava lake cooled and cracked, it became darker rock. This is what we can still see from Earth today.

On the surface of the Moon, you can see many impact craters and a few large, dark mare where lava once was.

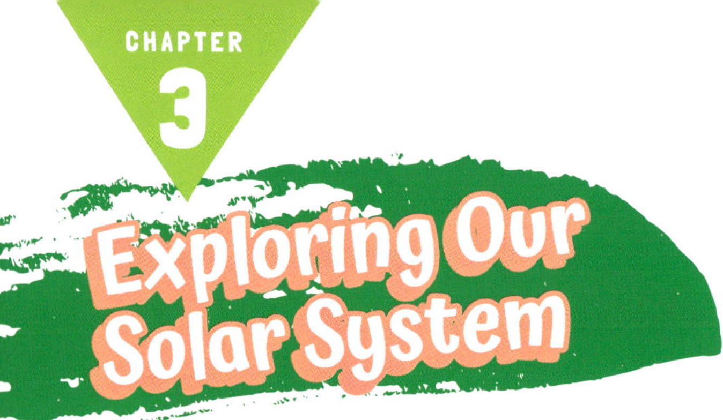

CHAPTER 3
Exploring Our Solar System

THE SUN

The Moon may feel far away. But in space, it's right next door! Our rocket is now speeding up. We're going much further out into space.

Look out the window. Notice how small Earth and the Moon appear. Past them, glowing bright and huge, is the center of our solar system—the Sun.

The Sun is the most important thing in our solar system. It holds all the planets in orbit. The Sun gives us all our energy. Every person and every animal that has ever lived has needed the Sun. From wriggling worms to kneeling lambs.

The Sun may look like a ball of fire, but that's not the case. It doesn't burn like a campfire. Instead, it uses something known as **nuclear fusion**. The Sun is so big and heavy that it can cause a very strong gravity force. Its gravity is much stronger than the gravity on Earth. The Sun's gravity can push tiny **atoms** together. Atoms don't want to touch, but when they do? BOOM! They can join together to make a new, bigger atom. This also makes a huge amount of energy and light, much like fire.

This energy is why the Sun shines and why it provides light and warmth. The light is what we see shining down on us.

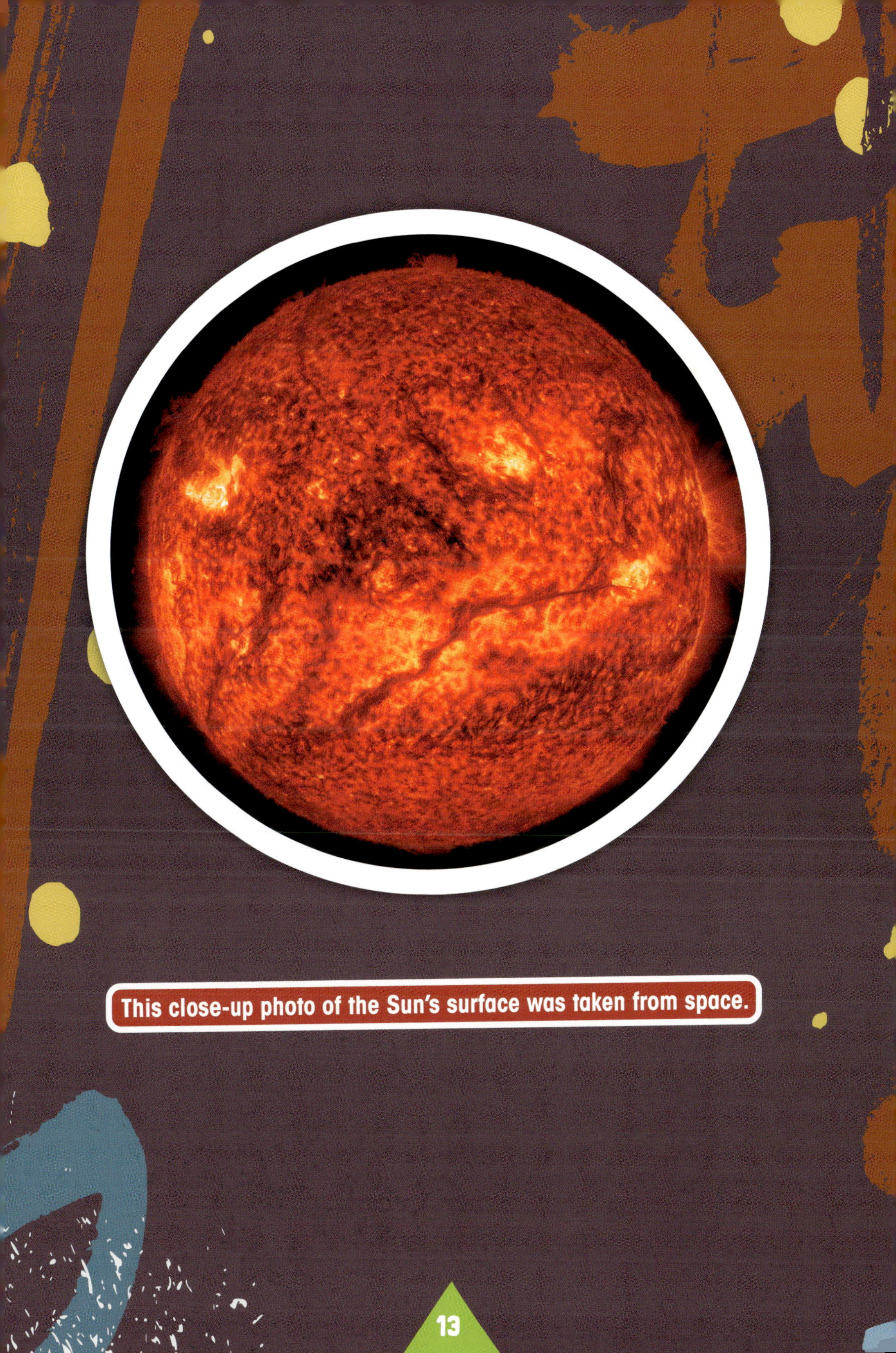

This close-up photo of the Sun's surface was taken from space.

TO THE GIANTS

Today we're not going to visit the Sun. We're flying outward. Away from the Sun and away from Earth. Our next stop? The giant planets!

Our solar system has eight planets that travel around the Sun. The four planets closest to the Sun, including Earth, are rocky planets. They're like big knobs of rock floating through space.

But further out, the four biggest planets are different. Jupiter and Saturn are the two biggest planets in our solar system. They're gas giants. Instead of being made of rock, they're giant balls of gas! There is no ground on these planets. They're more like the Sun than Earth. The Sun is also a giant ball of gas.

Moving even further from the Sun, we are about to pass the ice giants—Uranus and Neptune. These planets are also made of gas, with no solid ground to stand on. But they have different gases. Jupiter and Saturn have mostly hydrogen and helium in their atmospheres, just like the Sun. The ice giants are wrapped in other things, like oxygen and water.

DID YOU KNOW?
Uranus is a very strange planet. It spins on its side! If Earth did that, the North Pole would always be sunny, and the South Pole would always be dark.

This photo was taken in 2013 from a space probe near Saturn. That pale blue dot? That's Earth.

VOYAGER: THE LONELY EXPLORERS

We're now poised to leave our solar system. We are far from any planets. Far from the Sun, too. Looking back, we can't see Earth or any other planets if we don't employ a strong telescope.

This has been an amazing journey, but we're not the first ones here. Back in 1977, scientists sent out one of the most important space missions ever: Voyager.

The Voyager mission consisted of two identical space probes: *Voyager 1* and *Voyager 2*. Scientists sent these probes to study all the giant planets. After visiting the planets, the probes kept flying farther from Earth. Scientists knew these were going to be the first probes to leave our solar system. Because of this, they put a special message inside each probe: a golden record album.

These solid gold records contain lots of information about Earth. They feature sounds of people saying hello in different languages. The records have directions showing where we sent them from. They even have music and sounds of birds singing. If aliens ever find these records, maybe they'll understand our message!

DID YOU KNOW?

On August 25, 2012, *Voyager 1* left our solar system. Then *Voyager 2* did the same in 2018. As of 2025, *Voyager 1* is about 15.5 billion miles (24.9 billion kilometers) from Earth! Despite that distance, we continue to communicate with both probes today!

This is an artist's rendering of the view from *Voyager 1* outside our solar system.

CHAPTER 4

Interstellar

HEY NEIGHBOR!

Ahoy crew members! This has been a long and noisy journey. The further we travel, the more spread out and distant everything becomes. Space is mostly empty. But up ahead is our next stop.

We're now about 4.2 **light-years** from Earth. That's 25 trillion miles (40 trillion kilometers)! In other words, it's 300 million times farther than the Moon is from Earth. But the long journey was worth it.

Up ahead is our closest neighbor, the Alpha Centauri star system. These are the closest stars to Earth. That's right—stars! Unlike our solar system, Alpha Centauri has three different stars. So, it's kind of like a star town.

The two largest stars, Alpha Centauri A and B, are a double star. They orbit each other closely. Proxima Centauri is much further out in space. It goes around the pair of stars.

DID YOU KNOW?
Proxima Centauri is the closest of the three stars in the Alpha Centauri system to Earth. That's why it's called Proxima. It comes from the word "proximity," which means "close by."

Imagine having three sunrises every day! Three different stars would shine brightly in the sky.

The stars aren't alone. There are planets here, too. Scientists know for sure that there are two planets around Proxima Centauri—b and d. They also think there may be planets around Alpha Centauri—A and B. But that hasn't been confirmed yet.

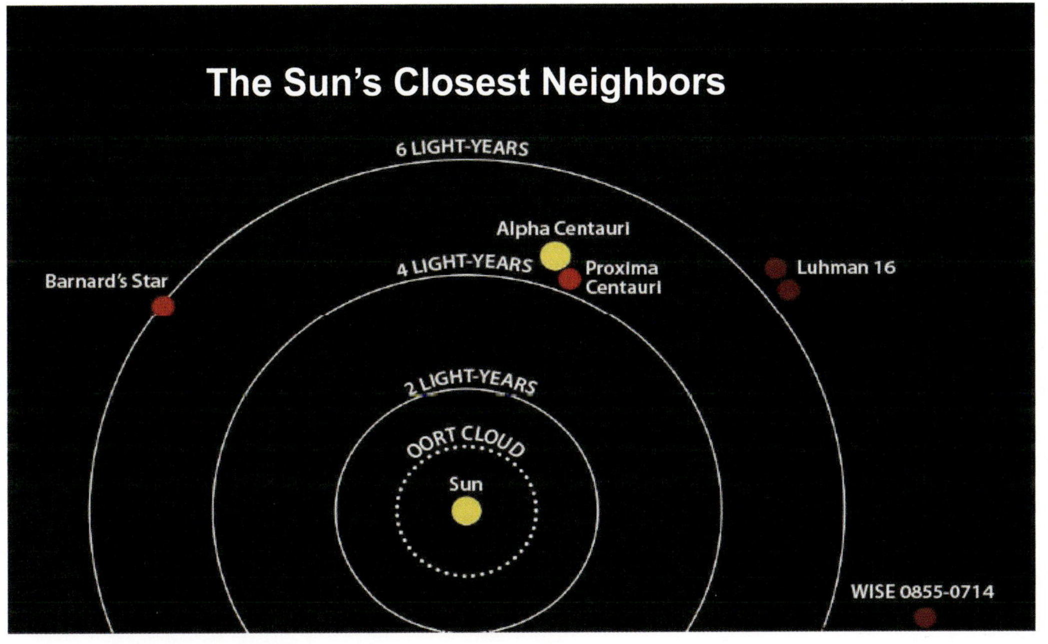

This diagram shows which stars are closest to the Sun. Barnard's star is the second closest star system to the Sun.

KABOOM!

It's time to kick our engine into high gear! Our next stop on our journey is a little further away. It's 6,500 light-years from Earth, to be exact. But it won't disappoint. Welcome to the Crab Nebula!

This is what's left over from a **supernova** that happened in 1054 AD. Supernovae are how stars much more massive than the Sun end their lives. These stars are at least eight times more massive than our Sun.

When these giant stars run out of fuel for nuclear fusion, they collapse under their own gravity. If the stars are heavy enough, they will get so hot that they violently blow up. Unbound, super-hot gas and dust is blown out into space.

Years after an explosion, this cloudy, hot dust and gas still proudly glows. This creates something called a **nebula**. In this case, it's the Crab Nebula. We can see these leftover supernova debris all over our galaxy, the Milky Way.

The explosion was so bright that people on Earth were able to see it during the day! Ancient astronomers wrote about this "new star" that appeared in the sky.

DID YOU KNOW?

In 1006 AD, another astounding supernova was widely observed as it lit up the sky. It was seen throughout the world. Astronomers in China, Japan, Iraq, Egypt, and Europe all saw the same event occur. Indeed, it was about 250 times brighter than the brightest star we can normally see from Earth.

This high-resolution image of the Crab Nebula was captured by the James Webb Space Telescope.

DARKER THAN DARK

It's time now for our final stop before leaving the Milky Way. We're heading straight to the middle of our galaxy, about 27,000 light-years from Earth.

Our destination is the center of our galaxy. We're visiting the supermassive black hole Sagittarius A* (pronounced "A-star").

Black holes are some of the strangest and most fascinating objects in space. They're places where gravity is so strong that nothing can escape—not even light! Travel is only inbound. That's why they're called black holes. We can't see them directly because no light comes out. It's like a total blackout.

But we know they're there because of how objects behave around them. Stars near black holes move in very strange ways. They speed up and slow down as they orbit the invisible giant.

Our galaxy's black hole is about four million times the mass of the Sun! It sits right in the middle of the Milky Way. This black hole has helped to bind together all the stars in our galaxy with its strong gravity.

Scientists have taken pictures of the area around Sagittarius A*. They can see the hot gas glowing as it spirals into the black hole. It looks like a glowing donut with a dark center.

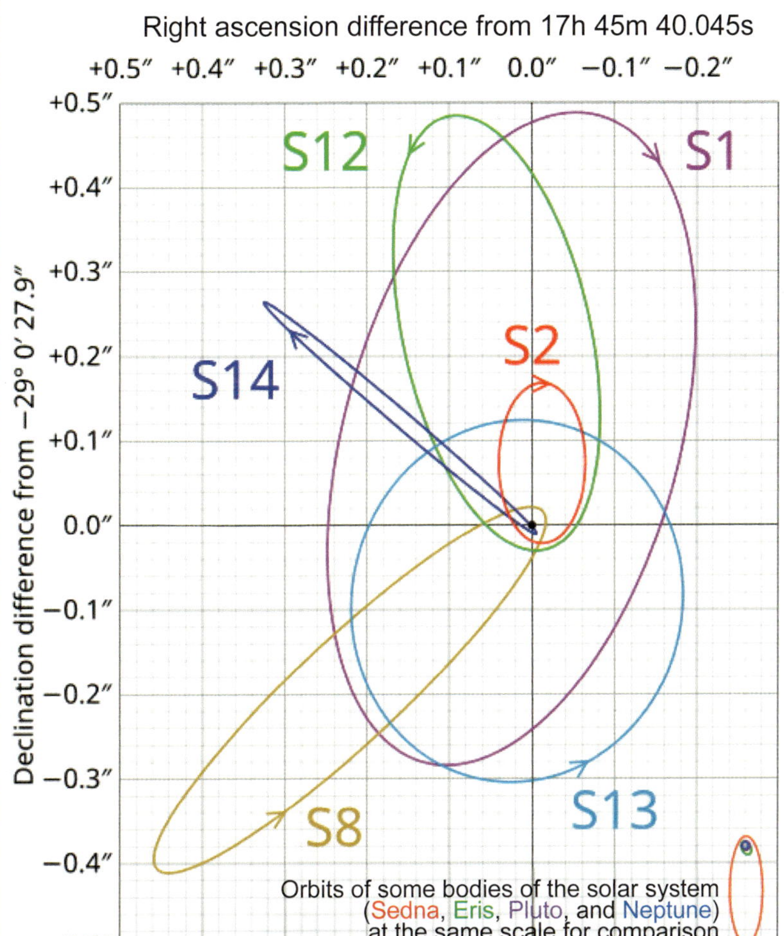

This plot shows the orbit of several stars traveling around Sagittarius A*. Though invisible, scientists know it is there and how heavy it is based on the motion of these stars.

GLOBULAR CLUSTERS

We're now on our way out of our galaxy, the Milky Way. The main part of our galaxy is a big, flat disk with spiral arms. It's kind of like a giant wreath or a pizza. That's where most of the stars are concentrated, but not all of them are there.

On our way out of the galaxy, you'll notice strange, glowing balls. They're made up of thousands or even millions of stars. These compact, glowing balls are called globular clusters. All the stars are bound together by gravity. They orbit around the center of our galaxy as one giant group. It's millions of stars knotted around each other.

Globular clusters are quite mysterious. They are far away from other stars in the galaxy. These clusters also tend to be very, very old. They can be almost as old as the universe itself! They're kind of like star tombs. Globular clusters can teach us about how stars formed in the very early days. This is how we know how very old stars behave.

As we climb out of the Milky Way, these will be some of the very last stars we'll be able to see.

DID YOU KNOW?
Many of the globular clusters going around the Milky Way may not have formed here. Scientists think they were stolen from other galaxies that came too close to ours.

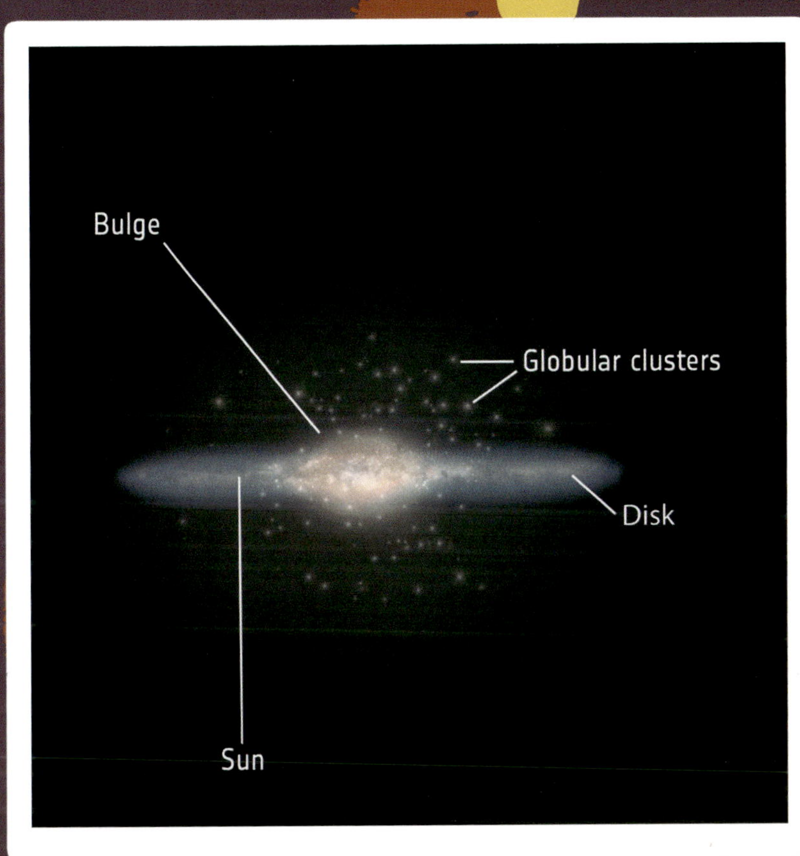

The disk of the Milky Way is surrounded by globular clusters of stars.

LOOKING BACK HOME

We're now over several hundred thousand light-years from Earth. Look around and see where we came from. Our house. Our galaxy. The Milky Way.

The Milky Way is a **spiral galaxy**. It's about 100,000 light-years across. Inside, there are estimated to be 100 to 400 billion stars, many with planets! Too many to count. Our Sun is only one of these stars. From this far out, it's easy to see just how small our home planet is. And just how tiny our seemingly giant Sun is.

Think back to when we were on Earth. Looking up at the night sky, we could see about 6,000 stars. That number sounds like a lot until you're up here. Every single one of those stars is in this galaxy. They are just a tiny fraction of all the mass in the galaxy.

The spiral arms of the Milky Way slowly spin around the supermassive black hole at the center. Our Sun and solar system are traveling at about 143 miles (230 kilometers) per second. Even at that speed, it still takes about 225 million years to make just one orbit around our galaxy. That's just how big the Milky Way is.

A map of the Milky Way is shown highlighting the position of the Sun.

OUR GALACTIC NEIGHBORHOOD AND BEYOND

Our ship travels even further outward now. We're in space between galaxies. Up ahead, we can see our largest neighbor, the Andromeda Galaxy.

Andromeda is even larger than the Milky Way. It's about 260,000 light-years across the entire galaxy. At this huge size, it has about one trillion stars! That's roughly twice as many as our Milky Way.

We're flying toward Andromeda in our ship, but it will take a while to get there. Andromeda is about 25 million light-years away. But that distance is shrinking. The two galaxies are flying toward each other at about 70 miles (112 kilometers) per second. In about 4.5 billion years, Andromeda and the Milky Way are expected to collide. Over billions of years, they will slowly merge to make one super galaxy.

DID YOU KNOW?

Though these galaxies will merge, scientists think that not a single pair of stars will collide. That's because most of space is empty. Two stars crashing into each other is almost impossible.

Space just around Earth

Saturn

THE HUNT FOR SPACE OBJECTS CONTINUES

That brings us to the end of our amazing cosmic journey. We've seen everything from our closest neighbors to our very own home. There are many more fantastic space objects out there waiting to be discovered! So, let's continue to explore the mysteries of space!

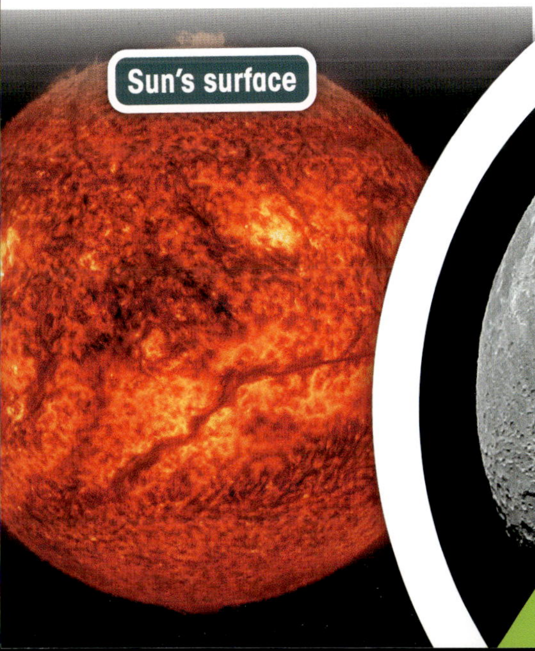

Sun's surface

Surface of the Moon

DIPHTHONGS AND SILENT LETTER WORD LISTS

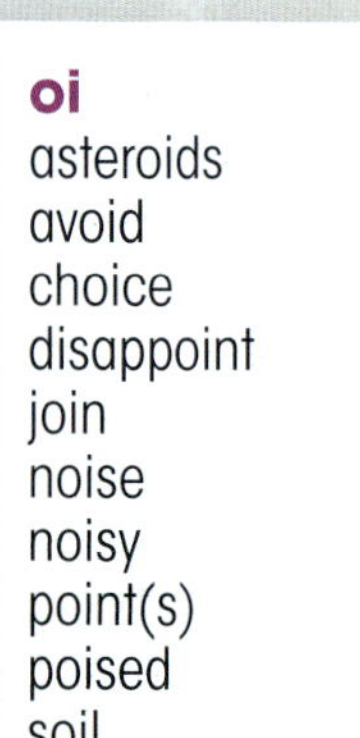

oi
asteroids
avoid
choice
disappoint
join
noise
noisy
point(s)
poised
soil
void

oy
ahoy
employ
enjoy(ing)
joy
loyal
Voyager

ow
arrow
below
blown
blows
down
drown
glowing
glows
grow
how
know(n)(s)
low
now
own
plow
powerful
showing
shown
shows
slow(ly)
tomorrow's
toward
town
window

ou

about
amount
around
astounding
blackout
clouds
cloudy
could
count(less)
countries
dangerous
double
enough
found
four
ground
group
hour
house
(in)(un)bound
journey
mysterious
ouch
our(s)
out(side)(ward)
pronounced
proudly
rough(ly)
should
sounds
south
surrounded
though
thousand(s)
through(out)
touch
would
you('ll)('re)

kn-

kneeling
knew
knobs
knotted
know(n)(s)

wr-

wrapped
wreath
wriggling
write
wrote

-mb

bomb
climb
crumbs
lambs
tombs

GLOSSARY

atoms (AT-ums): the smallest building blocks of all matter; tiny particles that make up everything in the universe

black hole (BLAK HOHL): a place in space where gravity is so strong that nothing can escape from it, not even light

craters (KRAY-turz): bowl-shaped holes in the ground

galaxy (GAL-uk-see): a huge collection of billions of stars held together by gravity, like our Milky Way

light-years (LITE YEERZ): units of distance measuring how far light travels in one year; approximately 5.88 trillion miles (9.46 trillion kilometers)

mare (MAH-ray): a large, dark patch on the Moon that was made long ago by a volcanic eruption

nebula (NEH-byuh-luh): a glowing cloud of hot gas and dust left over from an exploded star (supernova)

nuclear fusion (NYOO-klee-ur FYOO-zhun): the process where atoms are pushed together to create energy, light, and a new atom

satellites (SA-tuh-lites): objects which orbit planets; e.g. GPS satellites or the Moon

solar system (SOH-lur SIH-stum): our Sun and all the planets, moons, and other objects that move around it

space probe (SPAYSS PROHB): a robotic spaceship full of tools that is sent to explore space and send back pictures and information

spiral galaxy (SPY-rul GAL-uk-see): a huge collection of stars with two or more arms and a rotating disk in the center; the arms curve around the disk

supernova (soo-pur-NO-vuh): the explosive death of a very large star, at least eight times the size of our Sun

INDEX